COVID-19 FOR KIDS

Understand the Coronavirus Disease and How to Stay Healthy

Written by
Catherine Cheung
& Elvin Too

Illustrated by
Christy Johnson

D1314956

Published with the support of The Majurity Trust's SG Strong Fund.

National Library Board, Singapore Cataloguing in Publication Data

Name(s): Cheung, Catherine Kaimen. | Too, Elvin Chien Kuoh, author. |
    Johnson, Christy, illustrator.
Title: COVID-19 for kids : understand the coronavirus disease and how to
    stay healthy / written by Catherine Cheung & Elvin Too ; illustrated by
    Christy Johnson.
Description: Singapore : Small Space Sprouts (Pte. Ltd.), [2020]
Identifier(s): OCN 1146012466 | ISBN 978-981-14-5477-6 (e-book) |
    ISBN 978-981-14-5534-6 (paperback)
Subject: LCSH: Coronavirus infections--Juvenile literature. | Coronavirus
    infections--Prevention--Juvenile literature. | Coronaviruses--Juvenile
    literature.
Classification: DDC 616.2--dc23

First Edition, April 2020.

DEDICATION

For Grandpa, Gong Gong and all healthcare workers helping the sick get better.

A portion of the profits from the sale of this book will be donated to the fight against COVID-19.

Find out more about this book, our donations, or what you can do to help at www.COVID19KidsBook.com.

Grandpa has a very strong will, but his body's weak and often ill.

A flu will keep him stuck in bed, with shivers, aches and a throbbing head.

A new virus has come to town.
Teeny tiny, it wears a crown.

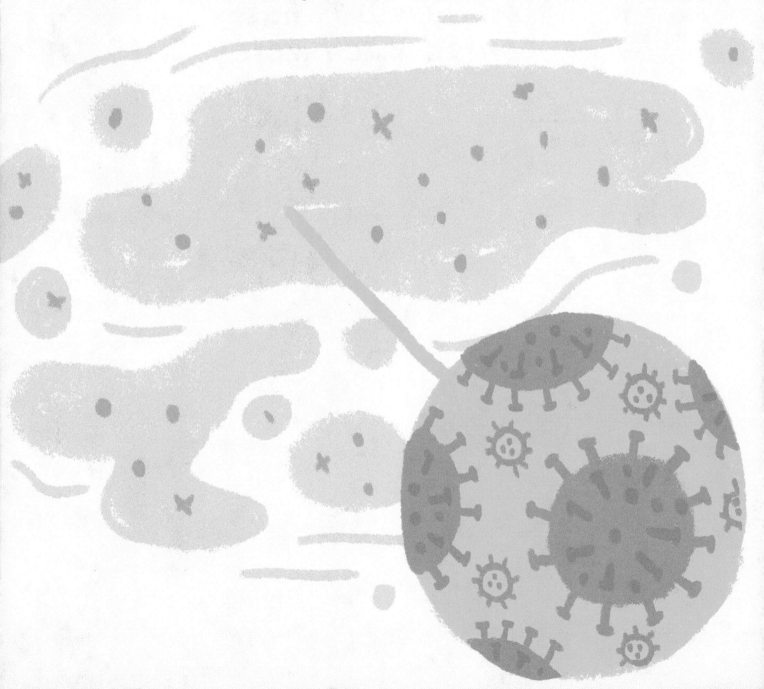

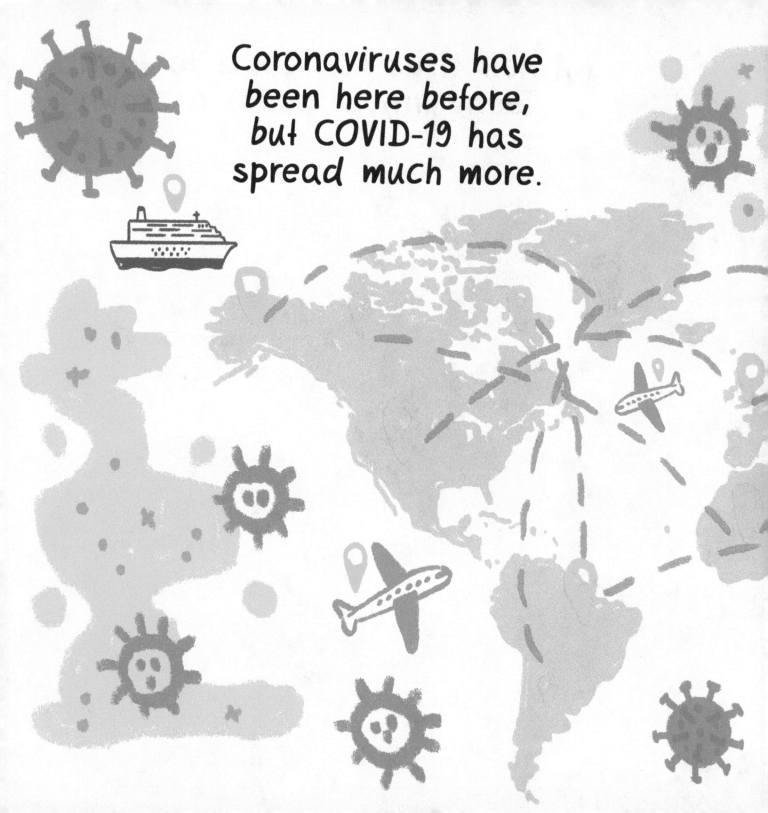

Coronaviruses have been here before, but COVID-19 has spread much more.

It's found a home
from Chile to China,
and hit Cologne to
South Carolina.

Catch it from someone's cough or sneeze.
If hands are dirty, it spreads with ease.

When many people are close together,
this sneaky disease
hops

with

pleasure.

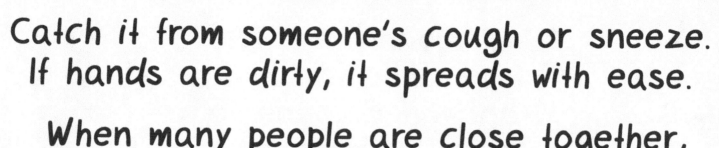

AH
CHOO!

If it gets you,
you might feel fine,
or a cough and fever
will give you a sign.

If it's bad, some have trouble breathing.
Maybe they'll need hospital healing.

We don't want Grandpa falling sick.
To fight this virus, what's the trick?

It all begins with me and you.
There's lots of things that kids can do.

Wash your hands often,
don't touch your face.
COVID-19 can be any place.

Use some tissues for a cough.

Stay at home when you're feeling sick.

Are you ready to
play your part?
Be clean and calm,
that's how you start.

Do it for Grandpa and those most at risk. Help them stay off the hospital list.

We may feel coronaviruses are scary.

But we'll get through this,
don't you worry!

BOOK DISCUSSION GUIDE

Now that you've read the book, let's talk about the coronavirus and COVID-19:

1. Do you know any older people, or people who get sick easily, just like the grandpa in the story?

2. How do you feel when you get a cold or a flu? What happens to your body when you get sick?

3. How would you describe COVID-19? What is it?

4. Why do you think people are so worried about the coronavirus?

5. How does COVID-19 spread?

6. How does hearing about COVID-19 or coronavirus make you feel? Why?

7. What can you do to stay healthy?

8. What can you do to spread fewer germs?

9. How does staying healthy yourself help others stay healthy too?

10. What changes have you / we had to make because of this virus?

11. How do you think COVID-19 is affecting other people – our neighbours, our friends, other children in the world?

12. Do you have any other ideas of how you can help people affected by coronavirus?

Find more resources and learn how others are having coronavirus discussions with kids at www.COVID19KidsBook.com/resources.

IN MY OWN WORDS ACTIVITY

My name is _____

I live in _____

I am _____ years old.

I read this book with _____

COVID-19 / Coronavirus is _____

_____

COVID-19 / Coronavirus makes me feel _____

_____

_____

Our life is different now:

_____

_____

_____

_____

I know I can help by:

_____

_____

_____

_____

_____

ABOUT COVID-19

People started to notice that a new illness was making people very sick in Wuhan, a large city in China, at the end of 2019.

Scientists got to work and discovered the illness is caused by a new virus within the coronavirus family. Coronaviruses usually circulate among animals but sometimes can also infect people. SARS (severe acute respiratory syndrome) and MERS (Middle East respiratory syndrome) are serious diseases caused by other coronaviruses.

This new coronavirus was named the "severe acute respiratory syndrome coronavirus 2", or SARS-CoV-2 for short. It causes the coronavirus disease, or COVID-19 for short.

COVID-19 has spread very quickly and widely. It was declared a global pandemic by the World Health Organization ("WHO") on March 11, 2020. According to the WHO, you can catch COVID-19 from infected people through small droplets from their nose of mouth.

When somebody who has COVID-19 coughs or exhales, small droplets land all around them. You can catch COVID-19 by touching somewhere a droplet landed, then touching your own eyes, nose or mouth. You can also get COVID-19 from breathing in an infected person's small droplets when you are close to them.

The most common symptoms of COVID-19 are fever, tiredness and dry cough. Some infected people don't develop any symptoms or feel unwell. Most people recover without needing special treatment, but some become very ill and have difficulty breathing.

The WHO advises that you can reduce your chances of being infected or spreading COVID-19 by:
- Cleaning your hands regularly
- Keeping at least 1 meter/3 feet distance between you and anyone coughing or sneezing
- Trying not to touch your eyes, nose and mouth
- Covering your mouth and nose with your bent elbow or tissue when coughing or sneezing
- Staying home if you feel unwell

To find out more, please visit www.who.int.

CPSIA information can be obtained
at www.ICGtesting.com
Printed in the USA
LVHW020345290820
664254LV00017B/1304